CAKES AND PIES

COOKBOOK

Belongs to

....

....

....

Cakes and Pies Cookbook is one of eight books published as part of a larger collection designed to help you write your own recipes in one place and have them at hand when you cook your favorite dishes.

This **Special Collection** also includes:

- **SOUPS**
- **SALADS**
- **PASTRIES**
- **APPETIZERS**
- **DIET RECIPES**
- **OVEN RECIPES**
- **VEGAN RECIPES**

Table of Contents

Recipe

Page

Table of Contents

Recipe	Page

Table of Contents

Recipe	Page

Table of Contents

Recipe	Page

Table of Contents

Recipe	Page

Recipe:____

Prep time:_______   Cook time:_______   Servings:_______

Ingredients

Directions

Notes

Recipe:____

Prep time:________ Cook time:________ Servings:________

Ingredients	Directions

Notes

Recipe:____

Prep time:________ Cook time:________ Servings:________

Ingredients

Directions

Notes

Recipe:____

Prep time:_______   Cook time:_______   Servings:_______

Ingredients

Directions

Notes

Recipe:

Prep time:_______   Cook time:_______   Servings:_______

Ingredients

Directions

Notes

Recipe:_______________________________________

Prep time:________   Cook time:________   Servings:________

Ingredients

Directions

Notes

Recipe: _______________________

Prep time: _______   Cook time: _______   Servings: _______

Ingredients

Directions

Notes

Recipe:____

Prep time:________   Cook time:________   Servings:________

Ingredients

Directions

Notes

Recipe:____

Prep time:________ Cook time:________ Servings:________

Ingredients

Directions

Notes

Recipe:_________________________________

Prep time:_______ Cook time:_______ Servings:_______

Ingredients

Directions

Notes

Recipe:_______________________________________

Prep time:_______   Cook time:_______   Servings:_______

Ingredients

Directions

Notes

Recipe:____

Prep time:_________   Cook time:_________   Servings:_________

Ingredients

Directions

Notes

Recipe:____

Prep time:________   Cook time:________   Servings:________

Ingredients

Directions

Notes

Recipe:____

Prep time:_______   Cook time:_______   Servings:_______

Ingredients

Directions

Notes

Recipe:____

Prep time:________   Cook time:________   Servings:________

Ingredients

Directions

Notes

Recipe:____

Prep time:_______   Cook time:_______   Servings:_______

Ingredients	Directions

Notes

Recipe:_______________________________________

Prep time:_______   Cook time:_______   Servings:_______

Ingredients

Directions

Notes

Recipe:_______________________________________

Prep time:_______   Cook time:_______   Servings:_______

Ingredients

Directions

Notes

Recipe:____

Prep time:_______   Cook time:_______   Servings:_______

Ingredients

Directions

Notes

Recipe:____

Prep time:________   Cook time:________   Servings:________

Ingredients

Directions

Notes

Recipe:____

Prep time:_______   Cook time:_______   Servings:_______

Ingredients

Directions

Notes

Recipe:_______________________________________

Prep time:_______   Cook time:_______   Servings:_______

Ingredients

Directions

Notes

Recipe:____

Prep time:________   Cook time:________   Servings:________

Ingredients   ## Directions

Notes

Recipe:____

Prep time:________ Cook time:________ Servings:________

Ingredients

Directions

Notes

Recipe:____

Prep time:______   Cook time:______   Servings:______

Ingredients   ## Directions

Notes

Recipe:_______________________________________

Prep time:________   Cook time:________   Servings:________

Ingredients

Directions

Notes

Recipe:_______________________________________

Prep time:_______   Cook time:_______   Servings:_______

Ingredients

Directions

Notes

Recipe:_______________________________________

Prep time:_______ Cook time:_______ Servings:_______

Ingredients

Directions

Notes

Recipe:____

Prep time:________   Cook time:________   Servings:________

Ingredients

Directions

Notes

Recipe:__________________________________

Prep time:________   Cook time:________   Servings:________

Ingredients

Directions

Notes

Recipe:____

Prep time:________ Cook time:________ Servings:________

Ingredients

Directions

Notes

Recipe:____________________________________

Prep time:________ **Cook time:**________ **Servings:**________

Ingredients

Directions

Notes

Recipe:____

Prep time:________   Cook time:________   Servings:________

Ingredients

Directions

Notes

Recipe:____

Prep time:________   Cook time:________   Servings:________

Ingredients	Directions

Notes

Recipe:____

Prep time:________   Cook time:________   Servings:________

Ingredients

Directions

Notes

Recipe:_______________________________________

Prep time:________   Cook time:________   Servings:________

Ingredients

Directions

Notes

Recipe:____

Prep time:________   Cook time:________   Servings:________

Ingredients

Directions

Notes

Recipe:____

Prep time:________   Cook time:________   Servings:________

Ingredients

Directions

Notes

Recipe:____

Prep time:________ Cook time:________ Servings:________

Ingredients

Directions

Notes

Recipe:

Prep time:______ **Cook time:**______ **Servings:**______

Ingredients

Directions

Notes

Recipe:_______________________________________

Prep time:________   Cook time:________   Servings:________

Ingredients

Directions

Notes

Recipe:_______________________________________

Prep time:_______ Cook time:_______ Servings:_______

Ingredients

Directions

Notes

Recipe:____

Prep time:________   Cook time:________   Servings:________

Ingredients

Directions

Notes

Recipe:

Prep time: ______ **Cook time:** ______ **Servings:** ______

Ingredients

Directions

Notes

Recipe:____

Prep time:________   Cook time:________   Servings:________

Ingredients

Directions

Notes

Recipe:_____________________________________

Prep time:_______ Cook time:_______ Servings:_______

Ingredients

Directions

Notes

Recipe:____

Prep time:________   Cook time:________   Servings:________

Ingredients

Directions

Notes

Prep time:______   Cook time:______   Servings:______

Ingredients

Directions

Notes

Recipe:____

Prep time:________   Cook time:________   Servings:________

Ingredients	Directions

Notes

Recipe:

Prep time: **Cook time:** **Servings:**

Ingredients

Directions

Notes

Recipe:____

Prep time:_________ Cook time:_________ Servings:_________

Ingredients

Directions

Notes

Recipe:_______________________________________

Prep time:_______   Cook time:_______   Servings:_______

Ingredients	Directions

Notes

Recipe:____

Prep time:________   Cook time:________   Servings:________

Ingredients

Directions

Notes

Recipe:____

Prep time:________   Cook time:________   Servings:________

Ingredients

Directions

Notes

Recipe:_______________________________________

Prep time:_______   Cook time:_______   Servings:_______

Ingredients

Directions

Notes

Recipe:_______________________________________

Prep time:________   Cook time:________   Servings:________

Ingredients

Directions

Notes

Recipe:____

Prep time:________ Cook time:________ Servings:________

Ingredients

Directions

Notes

Recipe:________________________________

Prep time:______   Cook time:______   Servings:______

Ingredients   ## Directions

Notes

Recipe:____

Prep time:_______   Cook time:________   Servings:_______

Ingredients

Directions

Notes

Recipe:______________________________

Prep time:______ **Cook time:**______ **Servings:**______

Ingredients

Directions

Notes

Recipe:____

Prep time:_______   Cook time:_______   Servings:_______

Ingredients	Directions

Notes

Recipe:____

Prep time:________   Cook time:________   Servings:________

Ingredients

Directions

Notes

Recipe:____

Prep time:________   Cook time:________   Servings:________

Ingredients

Directions

Notes

Recipe:_______________________________________

Prep time:________   Cook time:________   Servings:________

Ingredients	Directions

Notes

Recipe:

Prep time:_______ Cook time:_______ Servings:_______

Ingredients

Directions

Notes

Recipe:____

Prep time:________   Cook time:________   Servings:________

Ingredients

Directions

Notes

Recipe:

Prep time:_______   Cook time:_______   Servings:_______

Ingredients

Directions

Notes

Recipe:____

Prep time:______   Cook time:______   Servings:______

| Ingredients | Directions |

Notes

Recipe:

Prep time:________   Cook time:________   Servings:________

Ingredients	Directions

Notes

Recipe:____

Prep time:________   Cook time:________   Servings:________

Ingredients

Directions

Notes

Recipe:____

Prep time:_________   Cook time:_________   Servings:_________

Ingredients

Directions

Notes

Recipe:____

Prep time:________   Cook time:________   Servings:________

Ingredients

Directions

Notes

Recipe:_______________________________

Prep time:_______ **Cook time:**_______ **Servings:**_______

Ingredients

Directions

Notes

Recipe:____

Prep time:________ Cook time:________ Servings:________

Ingredients

Directions

Notes

Recipe:

Prep time: _______ **Cook time:** _______ **Servings:** _______

Ingredients

Directions

Notes

Recipe:_______________________________

Prep time:______ Cook time:______ Servings:______

Ingredients

Directions

Notes

Recipe:____

Prep time:________   Cook time:________   Servings:________

Ingredients

Directions

Notes

Prep time:_______ Cook time:_______ Servings:_______

Ingredients

Directions

Notes

Recipe:_______________________________________

Prep time:_______   Cook time:_______   Servings:_______

Ingredients

Directions

Notes

Recipe:____

Prep time:_______   Cook time:_______   Servings:_______

<table>
<tr><th>Ingredients</th><th>Directions</th></tr>
</table>

Notes

Recipe:____

Prep time:________ Cook time:________ Servings:________

| Ingredients | Directions |

Notes

Recipe:____

Prep time:_______   Cook time:_______   Servings:_______

Ingredients

Directions

Notes

Recipe:____

Prep time:_______   Cook time:_______   Servings:_______

Ingredients

Directions

Notes

Recipe:_______________________________________

Prep time:_______   Cook time:_______   Servings:_______

Ingredients

Directions

Notes

Recipe:____

Prep time:_______   Cook time:_______   Servings:_______

Ingredients   ## Directions

Notes

Recipe:____

Prep time:________   Cook time:________   Servings:________

Ingredients

Directions

Notes

Recipe:_______________________________________

Prep time:_______ Cook time:_______ Servings:_______

Ingredients	Directions

Notes

Recipe:____

Prep time:_______   Cook time:_______   Servings:_______

Ingredients

Directions

Notes

Recipe:____

Prep time:_______   Cook time:_______   Servings:_______

| Ingredients | Directions |

Notes

Recipe:____

Prep time:________   Cook time:________   Servings:________

Ingredients

Directions

Notes

Recipe:

Prep time:______ **Cook time:**______ **Servings:**______

Ingredients	Directions

Notes

Recipe:____

Prep time:_________   Cook time:_________   Servings:_________

Ingredients

Directions

Notes

Recipe:_______________________________________

Prep time:________   Cook time:________   Servings:________

Ingredients

Directions

Notes

Recipe:____

Prep time:_______   Cook time:_______   Servings:_______

Ingredients

Directions

Notes

Recipe:____

Prep time:________   Cook time:________   Servings:________

Ingredients

Directions

Notes

Recipe:____

Prep time:_______   Cook time:_______   Servings:_______

Ingredients

Directions

Notes

Prep time:_______   Cook time:_______   Servings:_______

Ingredients

Directions

Notes

Recipe:____

Prep time:________   Cook time:________   Servings:________

Ingredients

Directions

Notes

Recipe:_______________________________________

Prep time:________   Cook time:________   Servings:________

Ingredients

Directions

Notes